Puffin Books
You Can Do the Cube

Can you do it? Or has Rubik's baffling cube defeated you too? No matter how much you fiddle and twiddle at random with the cube, you will never be able to return it to its original state. There are over 43 billion possible ways of arranging the pieces of Rubik's cube, so you need to have a method to get it back the way it began.

Thirteen-year-old Patrick Bossert has worked out this foolproof method of solving Rubik's cube. He takes you carefully through all the possible stages, with easy-to-follow instructions covering all the problems you might be faced with. It may take you longer than the minute-and-a-half it takes Patrick Bossert to solve the cube, but solve it you can, again and again.

Once you have solved your cube, try some of the fascinating patterns you can make with it, or use the detailed maintenance instructions to dismantle and improve the action of your cube.

Amaze your friends, astound your family with this infallible method of solving Rubik's cube. For adults and children – brainless or brilliant – whoever you are, YOU CAN DO THE CUBE!

Patrick Bossert

You Can Do the
the

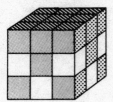

Cube

Puffin Books

Puffin Books, Penguin Books Ltd, Harmondsworth, Middlesex, England
Penguin Books, 625 Madison Avenue, New York, New York 10022, U.S.A.
Penguin Books Australia Ltd, Ringwood, Victoria, Australia
Penguin Books Canada Ltd, 2801 John Street, Markham, Ontario, Canada L3R 1B4
Penguin Books (N.Z.) Ltd, 182-190 Wairau Road, Auckland 10, New Zealand.

First published 1981 Reprinted 1981 (nine times)

Printed and bound in Great Britain by
Cox & Wyman Ltd, Reading
Set in Times

To my brilliant cousin, Joachim

Contents

Introduction

I have always been fascinated by three-dimensional objects and puzzles, so when a girl came to school one day with one of Rubik's cubes, which she had been sent from America, I was hooked. However, it was virtually impossible to find a cube for sale in this country at that time and I scoured all the likely shops without success, which was very frustrating. Then in February this year I went to stay with my grandmother in Switzerland and was delighted to find my cousin Joachim there as well, with a cube! Soon, every spare moment was taken up with this tantalizing and infuriating puzzle. Even when I broke my right hand skiing and was in plaster, it was still possible to hold the cube with the broken hand and twist with the other. Gradually we managed to work out the basic moves and five days later we had solved the cube!

Then it was time to come home and I still didn't have a cube of my own. We tried to find a cube in Berne but there was an acute shortage and eventually I had to give up. Before we left Switzerland, I ordered a cube from a shop in Berne and my grandmother sent it on to me in March.

By now there were several people in school who had the cube and we formed a club, swapping ideas for methods and challenging each other to cube contests. There seemed to be quite a demand for instructions on how to solve the cube, so I copied out some of my basic moves, to get people started, and sold them round the school and to friends. One of these sets of instructions fell into the hands of a boy whose father works for Penguin Books, and the next thing that happened was a surprise telephone call one evening from Puffin, asking me to write this book!

In the book, I have given you all the moves you will need to solve the cube my way. It will probably take you a while to solve the cube the first time, especially if it is new to you, but don't despair and don't give up. Once you have solved the cube it will become easier every time and you can start timing yourself to see how quickly you can do it.

I am sure that you will find the cube fascinating and I hope that you will have as much fun with it as I have had.

You can do the cube!

Richmond, June 1981

The Cube and How It Works

The baffling Rubik's Cube was invented by a Hungarian architect and designer, Ernö Rubik. He was trying to find some way of helping his students understand three-dimensional problems and came up with his cube. Rubik himself took over a month to solve his cube the first time and nobody knows how long his students took! Since then, the cube's popularity has spread world-wide and the millions of cubes produced have become one of Hungary's chief exports. Cube competitions have sprung up everywhere, with rival cubemasters trying to increase the speed at which they can solve the cube. The current record for solving the cube stands at twenty-four seconds, though no doubt that will soon be broken. No wonder that the cube has been dubbed 'the toy of the century'.

The cube's success is largely due to its ingenious internal mechanism, which is also surprisingly simple. The cube consists of twenty-six pieces, commonly known as cubelets, six of which are connected to the cube's core:

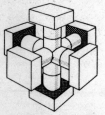

These six cubelets hold the other twenty cubelets in position.

There are eight corner piece cubelets, which have three coloured sides, and twelve edge piece cubelets, which have two coloured sides. Each of these cubelets has a 'foot', which hooks it into the central mechanism and keeps it firmly in place.

A corner piece cubelet   *An edge piece cubelet*

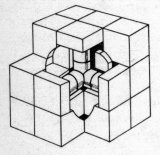

A cube with some cubelets removed to show the central mechanism

Cube Maintenance

You may find that your cube is very stiff to turn, in which case you will need to open it up and grease it a bit with some petroleum jelly, such as Vaseline.

To open up the cube, turn the top slice through 45°, and insert a medium-sized screwdriver under one of the edge pieces, like this:

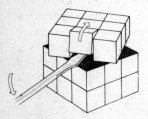

Apply a gentle pressure to the screwdriver until the edge piece pops out. The two loose corner pieces should then come out easily without any force. Keep the rest of the top slice in its 45° position and you should be able to reach into the centre of the cube and put a blob of Vaseline on to the mechanism.

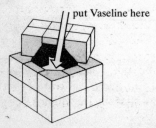

put Vaseline here

If you find that your cube has become too loose and falls apart easily, you should dismantle the whole cube so that you can get at the central mechanism on its own. Underneath each of the cubelets attached to the central mechanism there is a screw, concealed by a thin lid. These screws can be adjusted to make the cube's faces tighter or looser.

Extreme care must be taken when removing the lids of these cubelets as they snap very easily. Use a sharp knife to cut round the edge of the lid and gently lever it off. To tighten a face, turn the screw clockwise, and to loosen it, turn the screw anticlockwise.

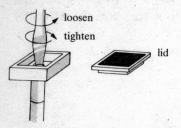

Some cheap imitation cubes have screws which gradually work their way out of the centre mechanism. Occasionally a screw will come out completely, making a whole face come off and fall apart. To get quick access to the screw in this situation, you should push the screw gently in against the lid, carefully forcing the lid off, like this:

The screw can then be put back into the central mechanism again, tightened up and the rest of the face reassembled. You may find that the lid will not fit tightly back on to a centre cubelet. If this happens, just stick it back on again with a small blob or two of a clear adhesive (UHU, Bostik or something similar, but not Superglue).

When you are putting your cube back together again, it is absolutely essential that you put all the pieces into their correct places, the right way up. If a piece is put back into the wrong place, you will never be able to solve the cube and the whole thing will have to be taken to bits again and reassembled properly.

To reassemble your cube, start with the bottom slice, then put the middle slice in and finish with the top slice. The last piece to go in must be an edge piece from the top slice. Turn the nearly completed top slice through 45° and hook the foot of the last edge piece under the top centre piece and push it down, like this:

Replacement sets of coloured stickers can now be bought from many stationers if the stickers on your cube become worn or ripped. You can also have great fun making your own stickers, using self-adhesive coloured paper, which will give your cube a truly individual touch!

Symbols

You will be able to solve Rubik's cube using the method described in this book, as each move you make is described by these simple, easy-to-follow symbols:

 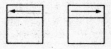

turn the top slice 90° to the left or right

turn the middle slice 90° to the left or right

 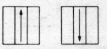

turn the bottom slice 90° to the left or right

turn the left slice 90° upwards or downwards

turn the middle slice 90° upwards or downwards

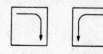

turn the right slice 90° upwards or downwards

turn the front slice 90° clockwise or anticlockwise

turn the centre slice 90° clockwise or anticlockwise

turn the back slice 90° clockwise or anticlockwise

 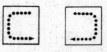

turn the front slice 180°

 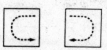

turn the centre slice 180°

turn the back slice 180°

The Stages

The best way of doing Rubik's cube is in five main stages:

Stage A 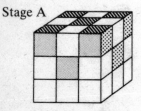 Choose which side you are working on and get its four corner pieces into their correct places, the right way up. *Tricks A1–A5*

Stage B 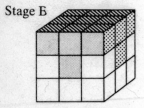 Complete the rest of the first side by moving its four edge pieces into their correct places, the right way up. *Tricks B1–B7*

Stage C 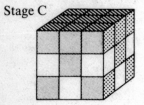 Get the remaining four corners of the cube into their correct places, the right way up. *Tricks C1–C4*

Stage D

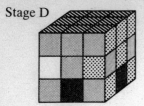

Move all the remaining edge pieces into their correct places, not worrying if some are the wrong way up. *Tricks D1–D12*

Stage E

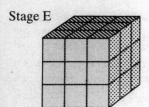

Rotate any edge pieces that are the wrong way up until they are the right way up. *Tricks E1–E5*

Important Handling Rules

It is important to remember that the colour of a face is set by the colour of the centre piece, since this piece can only be rotated, never moved out of its place.

Many people confuse themselves by holding the cube in a different way after turning a face. It is vital that the cube is held in the same way throughout all the moves for each trick, so that you don't lose the orientation of the cube. It often helps to remember the colour of the top and front centre pieces.

Make sure that the slices are always completely squared up with the cube before and after each move.

Sometimes you will find that you will manage to get a piece into the right place on the cube but that it is facing the wrong way up, like this:

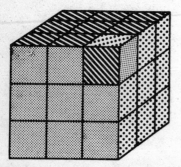

Don't worry about this as there is always a trick described for turning a piece the other way up, without moving it out of position, so that you end up with your piece in the right place the right way up, like this:

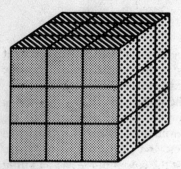

To Begin

The first thing that has to be done is to get one side of the cube into place (Stages A and B). Choose a colour to start with and find that colour's centre piece. Hold the cube so that this centre piece is on the top face, which we will call Side 1.

While you are getting the pieces of Side 1 into place, you can ignore what is happening to the rest of the cube. If a group of the same colour pieces appears accidentally elsewhere on the cube, ignore them as they will get mixed up again in the process of getting Side 1 correct.

Stage A

The next thing to be done is to get the corners of Side 1 into their correct places. Each corner piece can be identified by the colours of the centre pieces on the three sides that meet in its corner. An example is shown here:

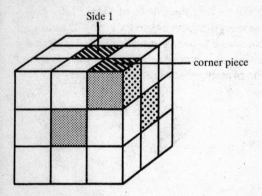

To get the first corner piece into its correct place, choose which corner you are aiming for, note the three colours involved and find the piece on the cube.

If the corner piece is on the bottom slice of the cube, turn it until the piece is directly underneath the corner you are aiming at.

If the corner piece is on Side 1 but in the wrong place, turn the slice it is in through 180°, to bring the piece on to the bottom of the cube. Once there, turn the bottom slice until the piece is directly underneath the corner you are aiming at.

When the corner is directly beneath its correct position, there are three different ways it could be facing and so three different ways of getting it into place. The diagrams below will help you decide which trick you should use.

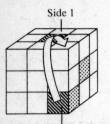

colour to go on Side 1

For this situation, use trick A1

colour to go on Side 1

For this situation, use trick A2

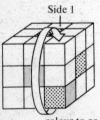

colour to go on Side 1 (on underside)

For this situation, use trick A3

24

If the corner piece is on Side 1 already, in the correct place but facing the wrong way up, it will need rotating within itself to bring the correct colour on to Side 1.

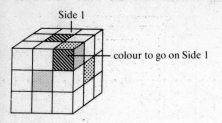

For this situation, use trick A4

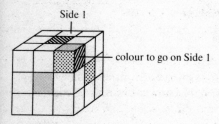

For this situation, use trick A5

Trick A1

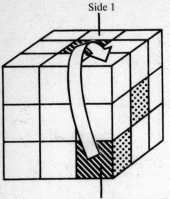

Side 1

colour to go on Side 1

Hold the cube as shown above, with the corner to go on Side 1 in the bottom right-hand corner facing you. Make the following moves:

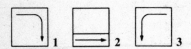

The corner should now be in its correct place.

This trick should only be used in Stage A

Trick A2

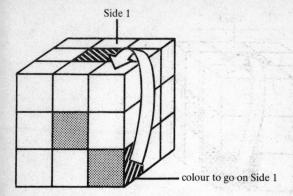

Side 1

colour to go on Side 1

Hold the cube as shown above, with the corner to go on
Side 1 in the bottom right-hand corner facing you. Make
the following moves:

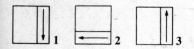

The corner should now be in its correct place.

This trick should only be used in Stage A

Trick A3

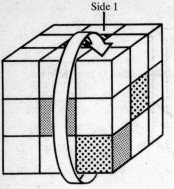

Side 1

colour to go on Side 1 (on underside)

Hold the cube as shown above, with the corner to go on Side 1 in the bottom right-hand corner facing you. Make the following moves:

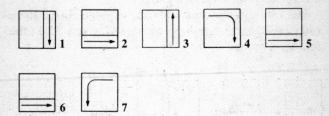

The corner should now be in its correct place.

This trick should only be used in Stage A

Trick A4

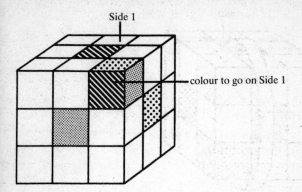

Side 1

colour to go on Side 1

If a corner is in the right place but with the Side 1 colour facing you, it will need rotating within itself so that the correct colour ends up on Side 1. If the Side 1 colour is on a side face of the cube, use trick A5.

Hold the cube as shown above, with the corner to be rotated in the top right-hand corner facing you. Make the following moves:

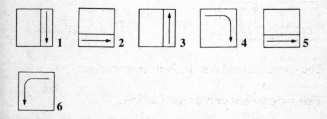

The corner should now be in its correct place.

This trick should only be used in Stage A

Trick A5

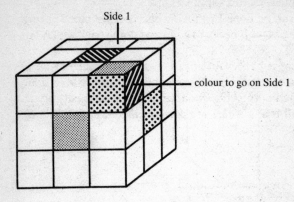

Side 1

colour to go on Side 1

If a corner is in the right place but with the Side 1 colour on a side face, it will need rotating within itself so that the correct colour ends up on Side 1.

Hold the cube as shown above, with the corner to be rotated in the top right-hand corner facing you. Make the following moves:

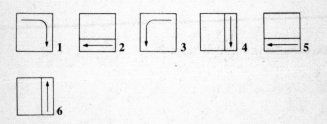

The corner should now be in its correct place.

This trick should only be used in Stage A

When you have got your first corner piece correctly into place, continue Stage A by getting the other three Side 1 corner pieces into their places.

This can be done by moving each corner piece in turn under the place it needs to go to and doing trick A1, A2 or A3.

You must be careful not to turn the top slice (Side 1) between tricks as this will move the corners you have done out of their correct places and confusion may easily occur. When all four corners are correct, the cube should look like this:

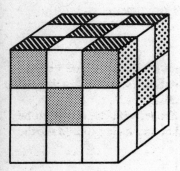

You can now proceed to Stage B.

Stage B

Now that Stage A is done, all that you have to do to complete Side 1 is to get its edge pieces correct, using tricks B1–B7. Each edge piece can be identified by the colours of the centre pieces on the two sides that meet at its edge. The Side 1 corners that you have already put into place will also help you decide which edge piece goes where. An example is shown here:

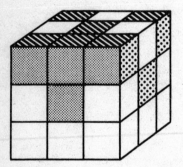

To get the first edge piece into its correct place, choose which edge on Side 1 you are aiming at, note the two colours involved and find that piece on the cube.

If the edge piece is on the bottom slice, turn the slice until the piece is directly underneath the place you are aiming at. The diagrams below will help you decide which trick you should use now.

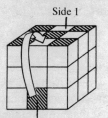

colour to go on Side 1

For this situation, use trick B1

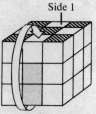

colour to go on Side 1 (on underside)

For this situation, use trick B2

If the edge piece is on one side of the cube, the diagrams below will help you decide which trick you should use.

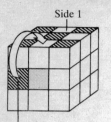 or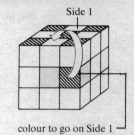

colour to go on Side 1   colour to go on Side 1

For this situation, use trick B3

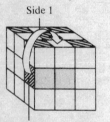 or

colour to go on Side 1   colour to go on Side 1

For this situation, use trick B4

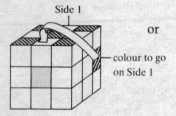 or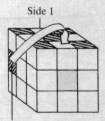

colour to go on Side 1

colour to go on Side 1

For this situation, use trick B5

If the edge piece is on Side 1 already, in the correct place but facing the wrong way up, it will need rotating within itself to bring the correct colour on to Side 1.

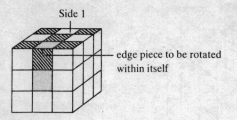

Side 1

edge piece to be rotated within itself

For this situation, use trick B6

If the edge piece is on Side 1 but in the wrong place, you will need to use trick B7 to bring it on to the bottom slice. Once there, you will be able to use either trick B1 or B2 to get it into its correct position on Side 1.

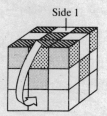

Side 1

For this situation, use trick B7, followed by trick B1 or B2

Trick B1

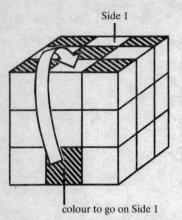

Side 1

colour to go on Side 1

Hold the cube as shown above, with the edge piece to go on Side 1 in the middle of the bottom row facing you. Make the following moves:

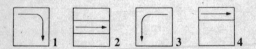

The edge piece should now be in its correct place.

This trick should only be used in Stage B

Trick B2

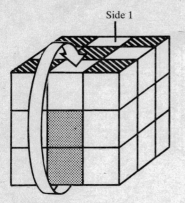

Side 1

colour to go on Side 1 (on underside)

Hold the cube as shown above, with the edge piece to go on Side 1 in the middle of the bottom row facing you. The colour to go on Side 1 is on the underside. Make the following moves:

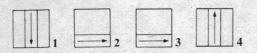

The edge piece should now be in its correct place.

This trick should only be used in Stage B

Trick B3

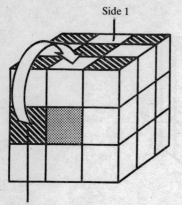

Side 1

colour to go on Side 1

Hold the cube as shown above, with the edge piece to go on Side 1 on the left edge of the middle row facing you. The colour to go on Side 1 is facing you. Make the following moves:

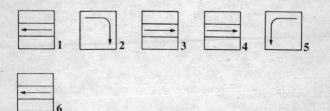

The edge piece should now be in its correct place.

If the edge piece to go on Side 1 is on the right edge of the middle row facing you, like this,

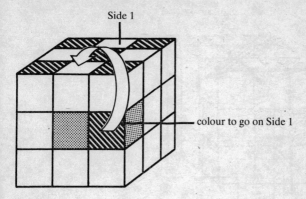

Side 1

colour to go on Side 1

just do the trick in the opposite direction. Hold the cube as shown above and make the following moves:

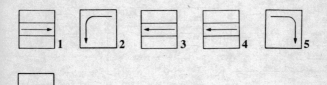

The edge piece should now be in its correct place.

This trick should only be used in Stage B

Trick B4

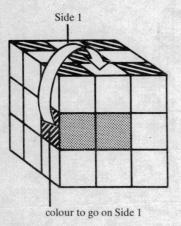

Side 1

colour to go on Side 1

Hold the cube as shown above, with the edge piece to go on Side 1 on the left edge of the middle row facing you. The colour to go on Side 1 is on the left side of the cube. Make the following moves:

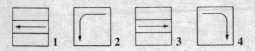

The edge piece should now be in its correct place.

If the edge piece to go on Side 1 is on the right edge of the middle row facing you, with the Side 1 colour on the right side, like this,

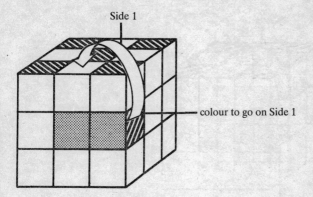

Side 1

colour to go on Side 1

just do the trick in the opposite direction. Hold the cube as shown above and make the following moves:

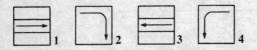

The edge piece should now be in its correct place.

This trick should only be used in Stage B

Trick B5

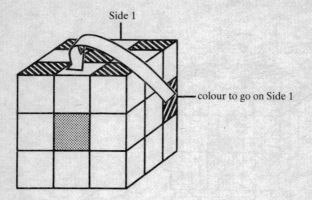

Hold the cube as shown above, with the edge piece to go on Side 1 on the back edge of the right side of the cube. Make the following moves:

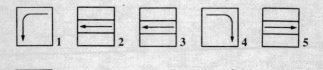

The edge piece should now be in its correct place.

If the edge piece to go on Side 1 is on the back edge of the left side of the cube, like this,

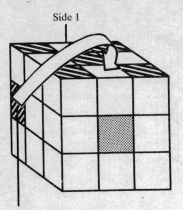

Side 1

colour to go on Side 1

just do the trick in the opposite direction. Hold the cube as shown above and make the following moves:

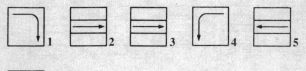

The edge piece should now be in its correct place. If it is in the correct place but with the wrong colour showing on Side 1, turn to trick B6.

This trick should only be used in Stage B

Trick B6

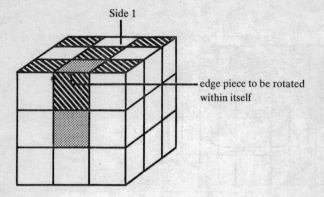

Side 1

edge piece to be rotated within itself

If an edge piece is in the right place on Side 1 but with the Side 1 colour facing you, it will need rotating within itself so that the correct colour ends up on Side 1.

Hold the cube as shown above and make the following moves:

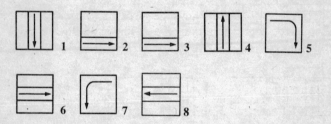

The edge piece should now be in its correct place.

This trick should only be used in Stage B

Trick B7

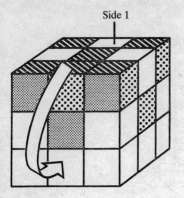

Side 1

If an edge piece is on Side 1 but in the wrong place, you should use trick B7 to move it on to the bottom slice. Once there, you will be able to turn the bottom slice until your edge piece is underneath its correct place on Side 1. Then you should use either trick B1 or B2 to get it into its correct position.

Trick B7 will move your edge piece on to the bottom slice of the cube. Hold the cube as shown and make the following moves:

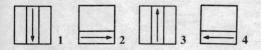

The edge piece should now be on the bottom slice.

This trick should only be used in Stage B

When you have got your first edge piece correctly into place, continue Stage B by getting the other three Side 1 edge pieces into their places, until the cube looks like this:

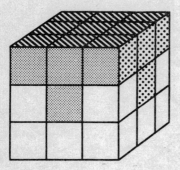

You can now proceed to Stage C.

Stage C

Now that you have completed Side 1, you can move on to tackle the opposite side, which we will call Side 2. Holding the cube with Side 1 at the top, Side 2 is at the bottom.

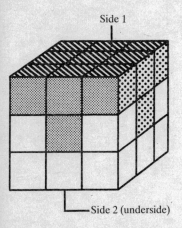

Side 1

Side 2 (underside)

In Stage C, you are aiming to get the four corners of Side 2 into place and the right way up.

First of all, you want to get at least two of the four corner pieces into their correct places on Side 2. You can do this by repeating trick C1 until two adjacent corner pieces have the right colour showing on Side 2. Then turn the Side 2 slice until one, if not both, of the corner pieces is in its correct place.

When you have one Side 2 corner piece correctly in place, you can use trick C2 to move the other three corner pieces into their correct places. It doesn't matter at this point if the corner pieces are the wrong way up provided that they are in place.

When you have two Side 2 corner pieces correctly in place, you can use trick C3 to swap over the other two corner pieces.

When you have got all the corner pieces into their correct places on Side 2, some of them may need rotating within themselves to bring the correct colour on to Side 2. Use trick C4 for this.

Be careful not to rotate the Side 2 slice between tricks as this may easily confuse you.

Trick C1

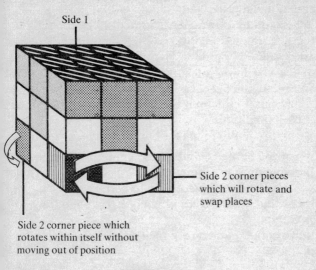

Side 1

Side 2 corner pieces which will rotate and swap places

Side 2 corner piece which rotates within itself without moving out of position

Hold the cube as shown above, with Side 1 on top and Side 2 underneath. As you hold the cube as shown, the two bottom corner pieces facing you will swap places. One of them will also rotate, bringing a different colour on to Side 2. The back left-hand corner piece will rotate within itself but will not change position. The back right-hand corner piece (not visible on the diagram) does not move at all.

You can use this trick on any of the four Side 2 corner pieces until at least two of them have the correct colour showing on Side 2.

The following moves can be made as often as you like to bring Side 2 corners into the required places:

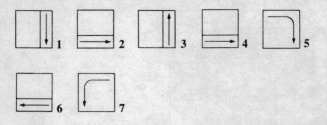

When you have at least two corner pieces showing the right colour on Side 2, turn the Side 2 slice until one (if not more) of these corner pieces is in its correct place.

If only one corner piece is in its correct place, turn to trick C2.

If two corner pieces are in their correct places, turn to trick C3.

Trick C2

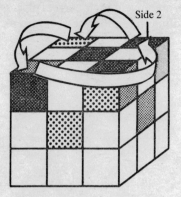

Side 1 (on underside)

This trick will make three Side 2 corners change places in the way shown above. Hold the cube with Side 1 underneath the cube and Side 2 on top. The one correct corner on Side 2, which will not change places, must be held in the top right-hand corner facing you. Make the following moves:

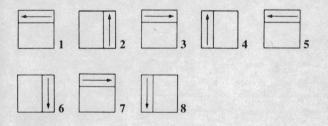

The three corner pieces should now have changed places.

If all three corner pieces are still in the wrong places, repeat this trick.

If two corner pieces are now in their correct places but the other two are still out of position, turn to trick C3.

If all four corner pieces are now in their correct places but two of them need rotating within themselves, turn to trick C4.

If all four corner pieces are in their correct places and the right way up, proceed to Stage D.

Trick C3

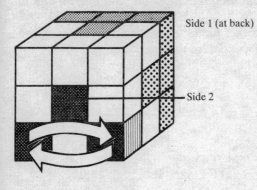

Side 1 (at back)

Side 2

To swap over two Side 2 corner pieces without destroying
Side 1, hold the cube as shown above, with the two corner
pieces you are dealing with in the bottom front row facing
you. These pieces may or may not have the correct colour
showing on Side 2. Side 1 is at the back and Side 2 is facing
you. Make the moves shown on the following page.

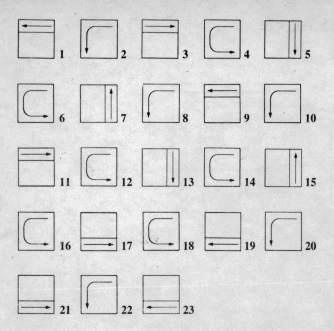

The corner pieces should now have changed places.

Trick C4

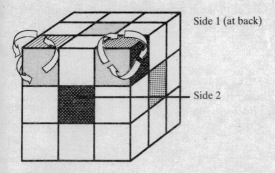

Side 1 (at back)

Side 2

If you have two corners on Side 2 in their correct places but with the wrong colour showing on Side 2, they will need rotating within themselves.

Hold the cube as shown above, with Side 1 at the back and Side 2 facing you. The two corners to be rotated should be in the top front row facing you. Make the following moves:

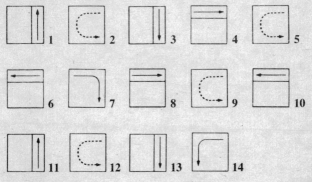

The corner pieces should now have rotated within themselves. You may find that these pieces are still not showing the right colour on Side 2. This is because the trick only turns the corner pieces in one direction, so you may need to repeat all the moves once again to bring the correct colour on to Side 2.

Using the tricks in this section, you should be able to get all four corners on Side 2 into their correct places. The cube should now look like this:

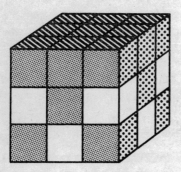

You can now proceed to Stage D.

Stage D

There are now only eight edge pieces left to get into place on your cube. The tricks in this stage will help you get all eight edge pieces into their correct places. It doesn't matter at this point if the edge pieces go into their correct places the wrong way up, as you will be able to rotate them later, using the tricks in Stage E.

There are a number of different situations that the remaining edge pieces could be in, which may be confusing at first. There are, in fact, only three basic tricks used in this section, the Sixer Trick, the Three-in-a-Row Trick and the Triangular Trick, which between them have been adapted for all the possible situations you might face.

Take this stage carefully and slowly in case you mess up the work you have already done. Start by identifying one edge piece and working out where it should go. Then look at the diagrams and find one trick that will make your edge piece move into the place you are aiming at. Don't worry for your first few moves about what is happening to the other edge pieces.

Then, as soon as you feel more confident about the kinds of moves you are making, you can look for two or three edge pieces that need moving and use the diagrams to discover which trick will move all of them at the same time.

Each time you complete a trick, come back to the diagrams and work out which trick you need to do next. Using a combination of these Stage D tricks, you should be able to move all the remaining edge pieces into their correct places. Don't worry if some of them are the wrong way up.

Make sure that you hold the cube in exactly the way that is shown in the diagram for each trick, otherwise you may disrupt the work you have done so far. You can use all these tricks on any of the faces of the cube, though you should always be aware of the position of Side 1, to avoid accidentally bringing one of its edge pieces into the trick you are doing.

The Sixer Trick

   or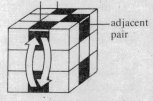

opposite pairs to be swapped over

adjacent pair

For this situation, use trick D1

The Three-in-a-Row Trick

   or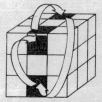

For this situation, use trick D2

58

or
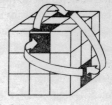

For this situation, use trick D3

or

For this situation, use trick D4

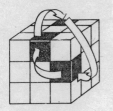
or

For this situation, use trick D5

or
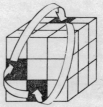

For this situation, use trick D6

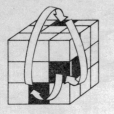
or
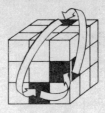

For this situation, use trick D7

or

For this situation, use trick D8

or
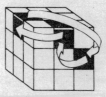

For this situation, use trick D9

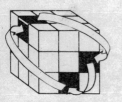
or
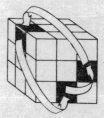

For this situation, use trick D10

For this situation, use trick D11

The Triangular Trick

 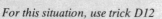 

For this situation, use trick D12

Trick D1

The Sixer Trick

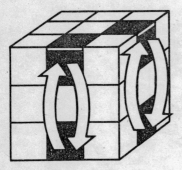

This trick swaps over two pairs of edge pieces on adjacent sides of the cube, as shown above. Hold the cube as shown and make the following moves:

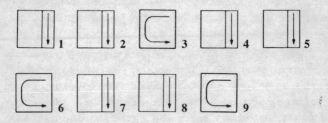

The edge pieces in both pairs should now have changed places.

If you want to swap over two pairs of edge pieces on opposite sides of the cube, hold the cube as shown here,

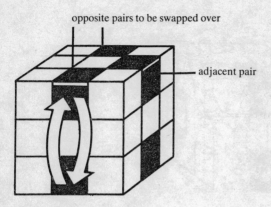

opposite pairs to be swapped over

adjacent pair

and do the Sixer Trick twice, first with one of your two pairs and the pair on the adjacent side, then again with the pair on the adjacent side and your second pair. The two pairs on opposite sides will now have been swapped over and the adjacent pair will not have been disturbed.

This trick is called the Sixer Trick because it is made up of six turns of 180° in two axes. If you want to speed this trick up and make it look really spectacular, hold the two adjacent pairs between your thumbs and forefingers, thumbs on the top pieces and forefingers on the bottom pieces. Then turn both faces alternately, without removing your thumbs and forefingers, 180° forwards, 180° back, 180° forwards. This takes some time to master, but is worth learning.

Trick D2

The Three-in-a-Row Trick

This trick moves three edge pieces in the same slice in the direction shown above. The fourth edge piece in the slice does not move. Hold the cube as shown and make the following moves:

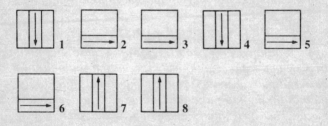

All three edge pieces should now have moved round.

If you want to move the same pieces in the opposite direction, like this,

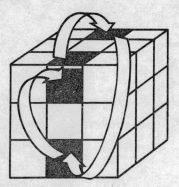

hold the cube as shown above and make the following moves:

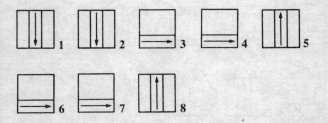

The three edge pieces should now have changed places.

Trick D3

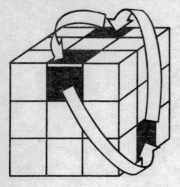

Hold the cube as shown above and make the following moves:

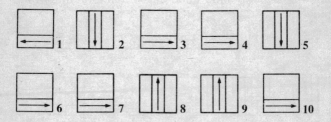

The three edge pieces should now have changed places.

If you want to move the same edge pieces in the opposite direction, like this,

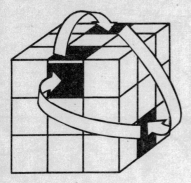

hold the cube as shown above and make the following moves:

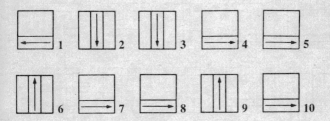

The three edge pieces should now have changed places.

Trick D4

Hold the cube as shown above and make the following moves:

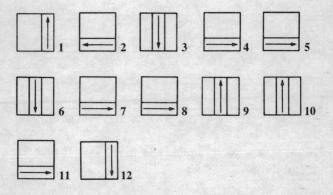

The three edge pieces should now have changed places.

If you want to move the same edge pieces in the opposite direction, like this,

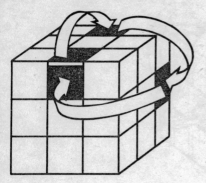

hold the cube as shown above and make the following moves:

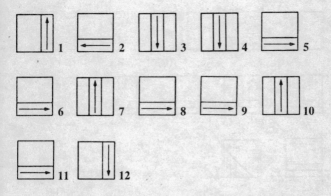

The three edge pieces should now have changed places.

Trick D5

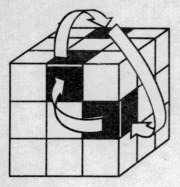

Hold the cube as shown above and make the following moves:

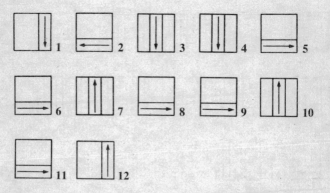

The three edge pieces should now have changed places.

If you want to move the same edge pieces in the opposite direction, like this,

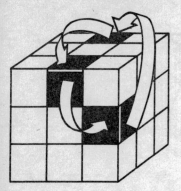

hold the cube as shown above and make the following moves:

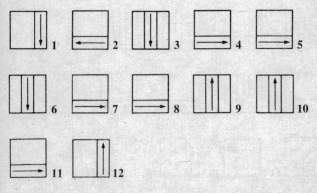

The three edge pieces should now have changed places.

Trick D6

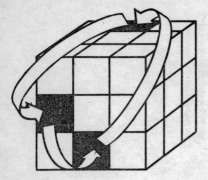

Hold the cube as shown above and make the following moves:

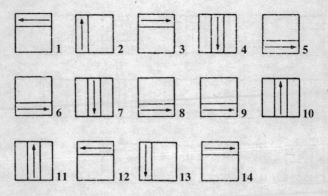

The three edge pieces should now have changed places.

If you want to move the same edge pieces in the opposite direction, like this,

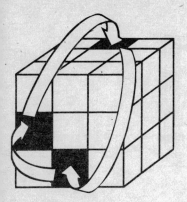

hold the cube as shown above and make the following moves:

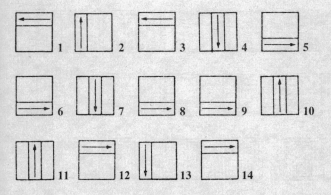

The three edge pieces should now have changed places.

Trick D7

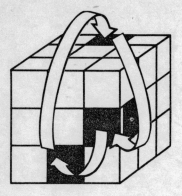

Hold the cube as shown above and make the following moves:

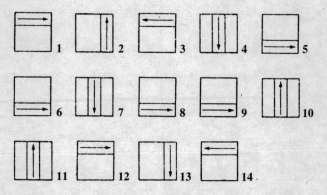

The three edge pieces should now have changed places.

If you want to move the same edge pieces in the opposite direction, like this,

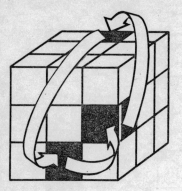

hold the cube as shown above and make the following moves:

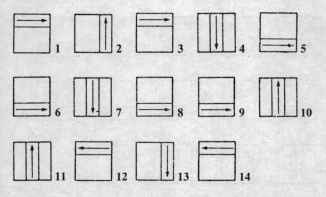

The three edge pieces should now have changed places.

Trick D8

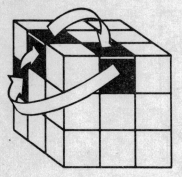

Hold the cube as shown above and make the following moves:

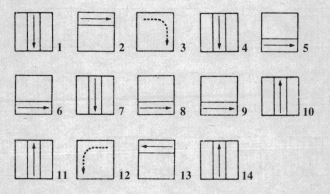

The three edge pieces should now have changed places.

If you want to move the same edge pieces in the opposite direction, like this,

hold the cube as shown above and make the following moves:

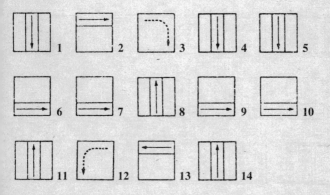

The three edge pieces should now have changed places.

Trick D9

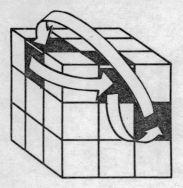

Hold the cube as shown above and make the following moves:

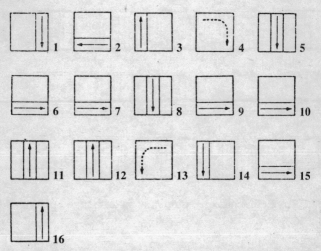

The three edge pieces should now have changed places.

If you want to move the same edge pieces in the opposite direction, like this,

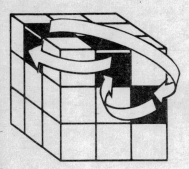

hold the cube as shown above and make the following moves:

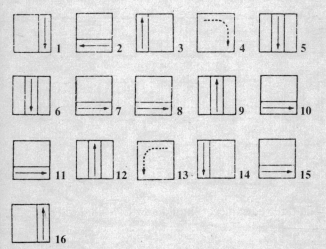

The three edge pieces should now have changed places.

Trick D10

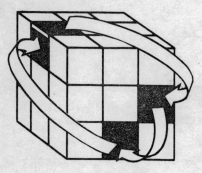

Hold the cube as shown above and make the following moves:

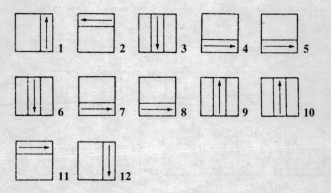

The three edge pieces should now have changed places.

If you want to move the same edge pieces in the opposite direction, like this,

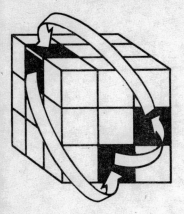

hold the cube as shown above and make the following moves:

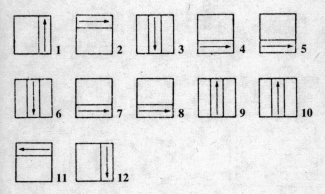

The three edge pieces should now have changed places.

Trick D11

Hold the cube as shown above and make the following moves:

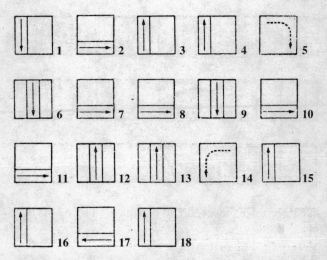

The three edge pieces should now have changed places.

If you want to move the same edge pieces in the opposite direction, like this,

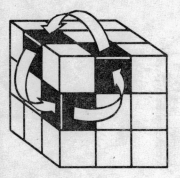

hold the cube as shown above and make the following moves:

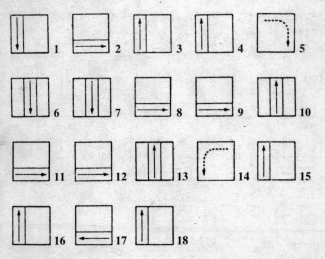

The three edge pieces should now have changed places.

Trick D12

The Triangular Trick

Hold the cube as shown above and make the following moves:

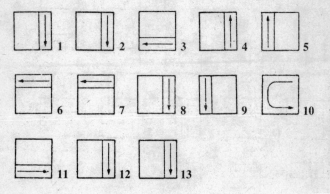

The three edge pieces should now have changed places.

If you want to move the same edge pieces in the opposite direction, like this,

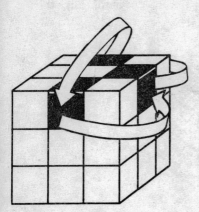

hold the cube as shown above and make the following moves:

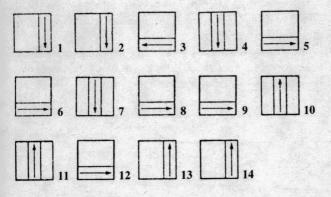

The three edge pieces should now have changed places.

Using some of the tricks in this stage, you should be able to get the remaining edge pieces into their correct places, though some of them may well go into place the wrong way up. Your cube will now look something like this:

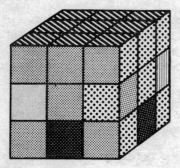

If some of the edge pieces need rotating within themselves to bring them the right way up, you should now proceed to Stage E.

If by lucky chance all your edge pieces have gone into their correct places the right way up, your cube will now be solved and you can congratulate yourself!

Stage E

You have done the hardest part of solving Rubik's cube by getting this far. This final stage is quite short and simple. The tricks in Stage E will rotate any edge pieces that you have got into their correct positions and will make them face the right way.

Use the diagrams to decide which tricks you need to do. When you have finished a trick, come back to the diagrams to decide which trick you should do next.

Make sure that you hold the cube exactly as is shown in the diagram for each trick, otherwise you are bound to disrupt your nearly completed cube.

There should always be an even number of edge pieces that need rotating at this point. If you have an odd number, you will never be able to complete the cube as it stands. There will only be an odd number of incorrect edge pieces if the cube has been taken apart and one piece has been inserted incorrectly. If this happens to you, turn to the section on 'Cube Maintenance' (page 13), take out the offending piece and put it back again correctly.

For this situation, use trick E1

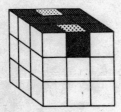

For this situation, use trick E2

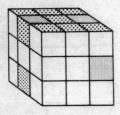

For this situation, use trick E3

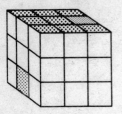

For this situation, use trick E4

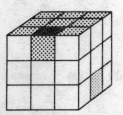

For this situation, use trick E5

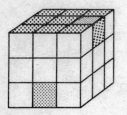

For this situation, use trick E6

Trick E1

Hold the cube as shown above and make the following moves:

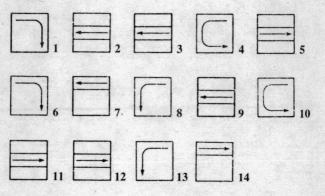

Both edge pieces should now be rotated within themselves.

Trick E2

Hold the cube as shown above and make the following moves:

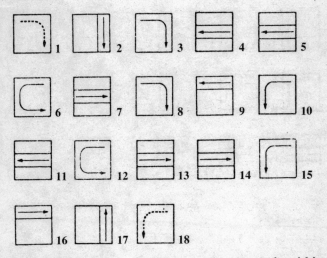

Both edge pieces should now be rotated within themselves.

Trick E3

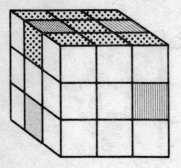

Hold the cube as shown above and make the following moves:

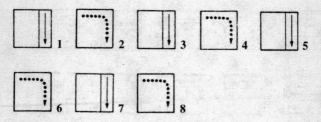

All four edge pieces should now be rotated within themselves.

Trick E4

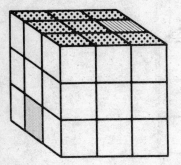

Hold the cube as shown above and make the following moves:

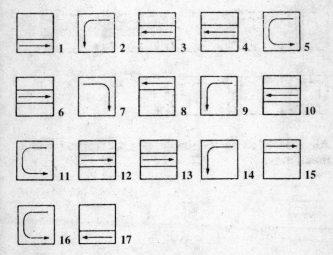

Both edge pieces should now be rotated within themselves.

Trick E5

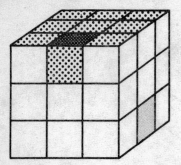

Hold the cube as shown above and make the following moves:

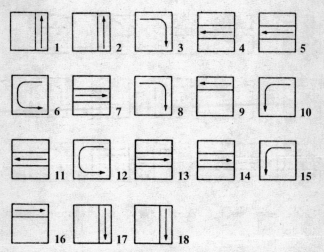

Both edge pieces should now be rotated within themselves.

Trick E6

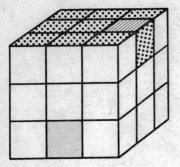

Hold the cube as shown above and make the following moves:

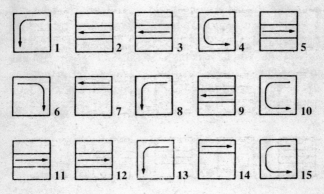

Both edge pieces should now be rotated within themselves.

By using the tricks in this final stage, you should now be able to complete the cube, so that it looks like this:

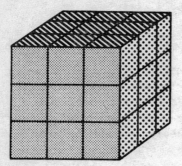

If you want to improve the speed with which you can complete the cube, you should try to learn the tricks by heart, so that you don't have to waste time by looking them up.

Now that you have completed the cube, you might like to try some of the fascinating range of patterns that you can achieve, some which are included in the next section of this book.

Other Patterns

Now that you can solve your cube, you might like to try arranging it into some of the interesting symmetrical patterns of which it is capable. There are a vast number of different patterns you can make, some of which are explained here. When you have tried all these patterns you can try working out your own, using the tricks and moves you have learned so far. Trick D1, the Sixer Trick, is particularly useful for making symmetrical patterns.

When making a pattern you must start with a completed cube, otherwise you will get into a terrible muddle and the pattern will not work.

Checks

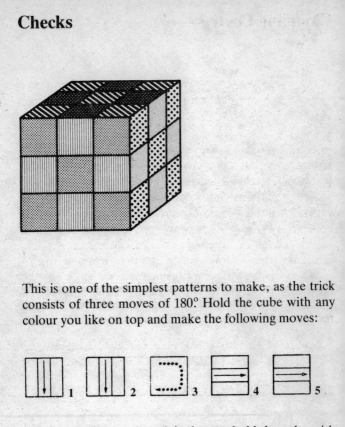

This is one of the simplest patterns to make, as the trick consists of three moves of 180°. Hold the cube with any colour you like on top and make the following moves:

To get your cube to its original state, hold the cube with any side you like on top and make the same moves again.

Changing Centres

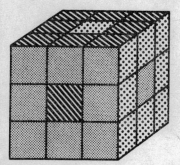

This trick moves all the cube's centre pieces round in a clockwise direction. Hold the cube any way up and make the following moves:

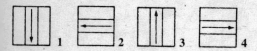

The centre pieces will move like this:

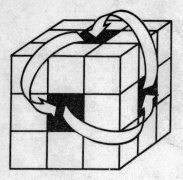

To get the cube back to its original state, make the same moves again, bearing in mind which way the centre pieces are going to move.

Vertical Stripes

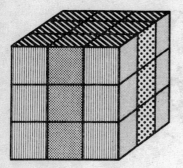

To create vertical stripes on four faces of your cube, hold
it any way up and make the moves shown on the following
page.

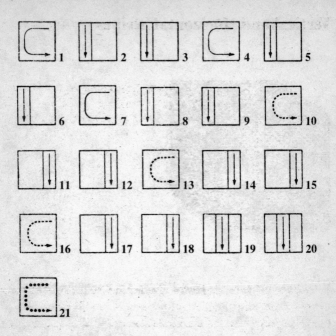

To get the cube back to its original state, hold it as shown above and repeat all the moves again.

Vertical and Horizontal Stripes

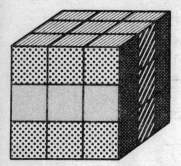

Hold the cube any way up and make the following moves:

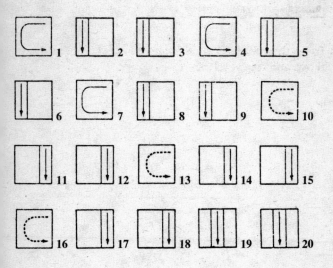

To get the cube back to its original state, you should hold the cube so that the stripes appear like this,

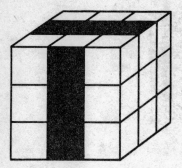

and make the same moves again.

Zig-zag

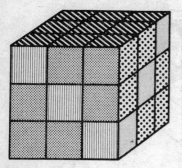

The Zig-zag forms a continuous line diagonally around your cube. Hold the cube any way up and make the following moves:

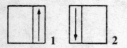

Holding the cube the same way up, turn the whole cube 90° anticlockwise in your hand. Repeat this combination of two moves and a turn five more times until the cube has a zig-zag pattern around it as shown above.

To get the cube back to its original state, hold the cube as shown and repeat all the moves and turns again.

S and Z

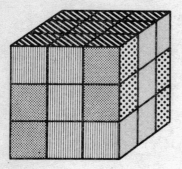

To get a continuous line going around your cube, forming S and Z shapes on four sides as shown above, hold the cube any way up and make the following moves:

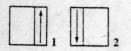

Holding the cube the same way up, turn the whole cube 90° anticlockwise in your hand. Repeat this combination of two moves and a turn five more times until you have the zig-zag pattern around the cube. Then, holding the cube the same way up, make the following moves:

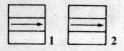

To get the cube back to its original state, hold it with the two plain faces top and bottom, as shown above, and repeat all the moves and turns again.

Six Hs

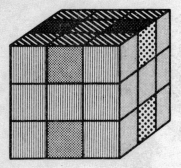

To get an H showing on every face of your cube, hold it
any way up and make the following moves:

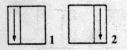

Holding the cube the same way up, turn the whole cube
90° anticlockwise in your hand. Repeat this combination
of two moves and a turn five more times until the cube
looks like the diagram on the opposite page.

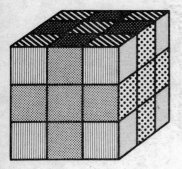

Hold the cube as shown above and make the following moves:

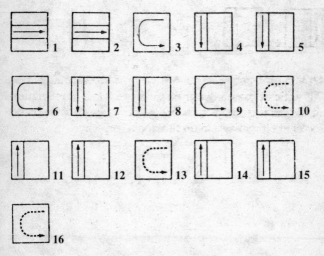

To get the cube back to its original state, hold it any way up and repeat all the moves for this pattern again.

Crosses

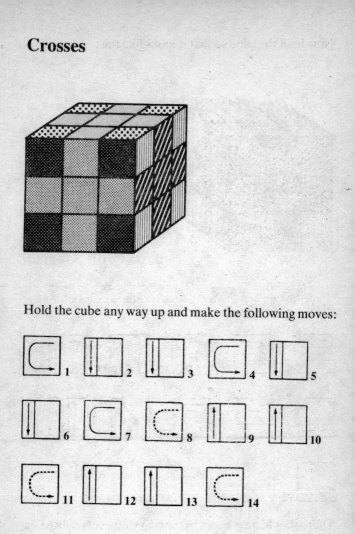

Hold the cube any way up and make the following moves:

Now hold the cube so that it looks like this:

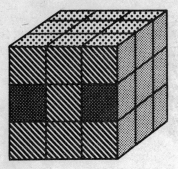

Make the following moves:

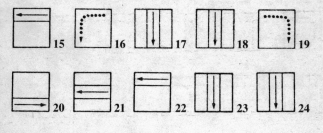

There should now be a cross showing on every side of the cube.

To get your cube back to its original state, it is vital that you hold the cube correctly. Hold the cube exactly as shown in the first diagram, making sure that the colours on the front face are different from the colours on the right side face. The top and bottom faces should have the same colours on them. Now do moves 15 to 25.

Then hold the cube exactly as shown below and do moves 1 to 14 again.

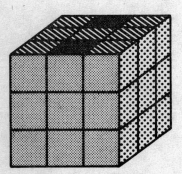